T0130115

Pantheon and Other Poems

Pantheon and Other Poems

Arnold Asrelsky ——————————————————————

iUniverse, Inc.
New York Bloomington

Pantheon and Other Poems

"For Han Shan and the Others" was previously published in *Tiger's Eye: A Journal of Poetry*.

iUniverse books may be ordered through booksellers or by contacting:

iUniverse
1663 Liberty Drive
Bloomington, IN 47403
www.iuniverse.com
1-800-Authors (1-800-288-4677)

Because of the dynamic nature of the Internet, any Web addresses or links contained in this book may have changed since publication and may no longer be valid. The views expressed in this work are solely those of the author and do not necessarily reflect the views of the publisher, and the publisher hereby disclaims any responsibility for them.

ISBN: 978-1-4401-6881-9 (pbk)
ISBN: 978-1-4401-6879-6 (cloth)
ISBN: 978-1-4401-6880-2 (ebook)

Library of Congress Communication Number: 2009935525

Printed in the United States of America

iUniverse rev. date: 9/4/09

For Hope,
my best reader,
best friend,
and loving wife

Contents

CLASSICS

Pantheon..3
Hades to Persephone 9
La Selva Oscura......................................11
For Lot's Wife and Orpheus 13
On a Performance of *Waiting for Godot*....................14
Little Red Archetype 15

THIS QUOTIDIAN LIFE

Only Goddesses Go Naked 19
Itch 20
On a Comforter Stolen
From a Communal Laundry.....................22
The Great Void.......................................24
Chios, 1999 / Lockerbie, 1988.................26
La Lanterna, Winter, 2007 27
Sex And The City.....................................28
The Ascetic..29
Two Homes...32
Metamorphosis (Continued from Ovid)..................33
Flies..34
Cougar at the Wildlife Conservancy..........................35
Recovery 36
Baldness 37

PEOPLE AND PERSONALITIES

Willem Claesz. Heda................................41
To Lewis Dodgson 42
Bernini's Portrait Bust of
Cardinal Scipione Borghese.....................43
Kathy 44
Small Winner 45
The Abortion...46

Secretary..47
Dad...48

ASIAN INFLUENCES

For Han Shan and the Others 51
To the Tune of Falling Plum Blossoms....................52
Travel 54
Summer Storm...55
Raga...56

SCIENCE

Entropy...61
In Praise of the Lens Grinders 62
Horoscope..64
Deus Absconditus...65

CONFRONTING GOD

The Abandoned Children 69
Eve's Soliloquy...70
A Footnote to *Paradise Lost* 71
The Tower Of Babel 72
The Golden Calf...73
Purification 74
The Desired..75
The Enlightened One...................................78
Eden...79

THE CRAFT

For Milton Gilman, Poet.............................83
Poetry...84

Notes 87

CLASSICS

PANTHEON

Zeus

To mistake the itch in the groin
for godliness and the upstanding prick
for a scepter of power
reveal what your creators worship.
What follows comes as naturally
as nor'easters and hurricanes
or the rapist's heaving buttocks.

Hera

My fault, I know, that I'm that comic trope,
The shrew in some celestial sit-com.
I could not stomach his so careless ploys
That reeked of arrogance and male power—
Him I could not touch, no, but them I stung
And whipped, the giddy girls he dropped as soon
His organ drooped, and he came back to me,
So smug and archly sly, it drove me mad.
So mad, I must confess in shame, that in
My rage I raised my hand against the babes
They bore, who am present at all marriages
And ease the labor women bear who bring
Forth life. Who oversees the flocks and fields,
Whose tender care brings forth ripe grain, rich fruit
From teeming earth to gladden all men's hearts.
How easy, then, to twist a woman's soul
And make her monstrous, goddess or mortal,
To sin against herself, a friend to death.

Poseidon

You were always mean, puny, and few,
but at least you had a sense of awe,
and if you 'scaped death under dark skies,
you raised your salt-rimed rags to honor me.
But whales and seals held my seaward gaze
and now you are so many my veins are filled
with filth and my rich fields turned to deserts.
But you are a disease that damns itself,
and I prophecy your death.
The silences will return
broken only by the shriek of the gull, the whales' song,
and the roar of the waves on shores set free.

HADES

King am I of no country
where no pale shades lap blood;
no roller rolls no stone
nor no desire aches toward the arching fruit.
No pomegranate, no seeds,
no tears wet the cheeks of no queen.
No heroes tread the deathless asphodel
though all come at last to me,
an elegant fiction, one of many,
all powerless to negate my no.

Apollo and Dionysos

Apollo is the god of the hard line,
the straight-edge and compass,
pediment floating on columns, balance,
the formal garden, manners, and civility.
The ballet is his and baroque music.
Enthusiasts find him cold and unapproachable—
but without him, entropy wins and mess rules.

Dionysos is the god of darkness and secretions;
mucus, sweat, and sperm mark his presence.
His minions piss alcohol
and loose men from the boundaries of reason.
Women worship him, their protector and power giver,
and naked, they range fecund jungles in his honor
in gratitude for his terrifying gifts
of excess and ecstasy.

No wonder when they meet, Dionysos sneers,
and his brother wears a look of disgust,
though both create genius.
And as each turns from the other,
mindful of his own lack,
their eyes lock in hate—and love.

Aphrodite

What should we have expected of her,
born of the cruel cut of the sickle,
of hot blood and sperm
and the cold salt foam of the sea?
Fatherless and motherless,
what should she know of kindness and care?
We worship her well
in our torment and despair.

Artemis

Sunlight and shadow dapple her naked breasts
as she and the man-hating huntresses
bathe in the fall's icy waters.
Her lovely arm tightens, tightens on the curving bow
and the shaft leaps longingly into the stag's heart.

Oh wounder of so many, what wound
do you bear as you wander pale, cold, and distant
through the dark night sky?

Hephaestus

A mother's boy flung savagely from heaven
by a father's rage, he limped from the fields
where the others danced and played.
He built the porticoes and towers
of fair Olympus and forged
the bolts of immeasurable power
but was ever haunted
by the beauty of straight-limbed Apollo
and the war-god's contemptuous laughter.

Ares, to His Supplicants

Compared to yours, Jove's thunders bleat.
The very atoms break in your fierce hate.
You have no need of me, now second-rate;
I learn my trade, submissive, at your feet.

ATHENA

Don't look for me in groves of Academe;
I am not of that bloodless tribe.
Remember, my owl's a predator, too,
and I bear the Aegis and helm of war.
My city did not breed pedants
but flaming meteors of men
whose blazing trail will never die.
The resourceful are mine, and the brave,
those who contrive well-spoken words
and clever deeds to win their way,
those who refuse to die before their death
and will not walk through life in sleep.

A PRAYER TO HERMES

Oh, God of boundaries,
come on winged feet,
ease and speed the crossing.

You, who love eloquence,
mark my service and repay me well.
Smile, gentle God, as you lead me
without fear, to rest.

ENVOI

Their temples lie open to the hot sun.
Only lizards lie on their altars.
They have been abandoned
like the lost toys of children
grown too wise to remember or care.
But they are immortal and live
where they always have.
Aphrodite looks out of a smile, a curl of hair;

Zeus sits at the kitchen table dispensing law.
They were always emblems
of the best and worst in us.
Now we have clothed them
in a jargon of therapy
denuded of beauty or magnificence
and are ourselves diminished.

HADES TO PERSEPHONE

Yes, my brothers made the better bargain.
Zeus wove his words and I was caught again.
He to peaks and wide sky and the other
to sea-roads where the seal and porpoise play.
The dim one to the darkness he deserved,
and armies of pale twittering ghosts.
They had Lethe, at least, and knew no loss.
Who could abide the dark, stale air? The dead
only, so mole took his black chariot
to Sicily to see again the sun.
Oh, that hot sun on my flesh, the warm air
in my lungs, flowery fields, grass beneath,
and in their midst, the fairest of all, you.
Field, flower, sun, all faded into you.
Should I have said, "Oh fair, lovely maiden,
I am lord of death: come to my kingdom,
be my sun and field and flower forever;
I will make you the queen of the shadows
of corpses"? No talker I, ever, less then.
Yes, I ravished you, but first you did me.
And when I pressed you to me, and you scorched
me like the sun, hot body against mine,
no words in my strangled throat but whimpers,
no thought in an empty head but the feel
of you, of you shuddering against me.
My heart, pounding as if it would burst,
opened a road to Hades and took you,
a terrified, shrieking child pressed against
a wall to escape the loathsome one who
had done this, and stung me, unaccustomed,
into honeyed words to soothe, make my suit,
and did, oh, miracle, did—and you sat
at this table we sit at now. I cut
the pomegranate you at first refused,
and each day cut again, refused again.
One day you looked into my sad face;

I saw, like a sun in this dark, dead land,
the hint of pity in your eyes, and my tears
wet my cheek. And when I took your small hand
in mine, it did not move. And now you smile
as you did then, at last, and shyly took
the seeds, and now tears again on my cheek
as you draw my head to your breast, and I,
having told the tale you love to hear,
embrace and lift you again from this table.
Tomorrow to my sister and glad earth,
but tonight to our couch, my queen, my love.

La Selva Oscura

Here the way is not lost
though the forest is as it was:
the gnarled branches still snag,
and the whip-like saplings
sting the pilgrim on his way.
The stiletto twigs still blind,
the shifting ground will heave,
and the sharp crack of the dead root
will signal your fall, as always.

In the distance you will hear
the lion's roar grow near,
and in the darkness, the lean wolf's eyes,
like dull red torches, follow still,
and the pard will insinuate her soft
shining pelt between your legs
as her growling purr
caresses and threatens.

And here, too, is your guide,
speaking all tongues to all travelers,
no need now to master his dead one.
He and all his friends are newly turned out,
annotated and explained to aid you
on your journey, wherever that may be.
Eagerly they will supply answers
and, even more eagerly, questions
that may beguile you on the tedious way.

There are also tales of a holy mountain,
of a hole that spirals to the center,
but all lands harbor such myths,
the inheritance of a more primitive time
held dear by a benighted people
to ensure fertility,
to secure immortality in imperishable
halls of feasting won by the brave and good.

As you slowly make your way,
you will discover the uncivilized terrain,
the wild and cluttered growth, created
by the intersection of innumerable paths
that cross and strive to hold their course
against the rival usurpers, but which have
right of way is now impossible to know,
but know no matter where you stand,
you are on a path, perhaps self-chosen,
perhaps bequeathed by parents whose
ancestors long ago laid down the route,
perhaps commanded by priest or Caesar.
But rest assured, you can never stray,
you are always on a path, a way
that leads inexorably on
to where the journeys end
and shadows deepen
and there is no hint of starlight
nor warm ray of a kindly sun.

For Lot's Wife and Orpheus

But looking back is what we do,
For we are now what happened once,
And what we wish flows from what's past.

The backward glance sees grief and loss,
The first as flames that freeze the soul,
The last as dark and deep as death.

On a Performance of Waiting for Godot

Knooks know the meaning:
we waste and pine
with stinking breath on rotting feet
despite our progress.
The night never comes
yet roars in like the whirlwind.
What shall we do?
Anything, nothing.
Fabricators of dreams,
inconsolable wraiths,
we shall keep our hour,
and will await Godot
and will not go,
although we shall be gone.
Good.

Little Red Archetype

Hey, Little Red,
what more to say of you,
heroine of a cautionary tale
to keep kids on the straight and narrow
and far from the dark woods
where the wild flowers are?

Darling of the analysts,
with bloody cap
signaling your readiness
as a not-so-innocent seductress
of wolves whose empty bellies
belie their true desire.

You seemed
good enough to eat,
and for him
(in some versions)
you were ready to strip
and crawl into bed
to be devoured, deflowered.

Your portraits are legion:
cherubic cheeks
and baby-blues
proclaim your innocence,
or you tip the reader the wink
from a face too arch and sly.

As capitalist icon
you have sold us cars,
luxury suites, and furs;
you have been a porno queen

and the heroine of film noire.
You are the virgin soul
on the brink of life,
and we see in you
our innocence lost,
and the price we paid
for the bargain made.

THIS QUOTIDIAN LIFE

ONLY GODDESSES GO NAKED

Only goddesses go naked,
fathered by a desire of mind.
Platonic archetypes of perfection
expressed in the smooth durabilities of marble,
they invite an innocent eye.

Perishable flesh is flawed,
breasts droop, skin blotches,
fat mars hip and haunch.
No matter—
the imperious needs
of bodily desire will have it,
though lust cannot take
its object straight,
demands it be decked
in the sly vocabulary of enticement:

Halters and harnesses,
translucencies that frame the forbidden,
the skirt that panders the knee,
the spike heel that slims the ankle,
swells the calf,
the perfume's rhetoric
denying the reek of decay,
the spice of paint
that renders flesh palatable.

All the multitudinous stratagems
of that primal leaf
born of a blush
that ever fixed the gaze just there
where what is hidden
seduces the mind's eye to create
what can never exist in this world.

No wonder we take our ecstasies with eyes shut.

ITCH

Demanding as a caterwauling infant,
yet without the grating on the nerves,
the itch is sweet to scratch.
A leg released from its cast
sets up an unheard howl
demanding the instant attention
of ten claws feverishly raking the sloughing skin
until a nurse dowses this dermic five-alarmer
in alcohol that instantly ends the fun.

In Rome a speeding truck hauls to the curb,
its driver drops from his high perch
and claws contentedly at his crotch,
his face suffused with angelic ecstasy,
(one of the simple pleasures of the poor).
Cuban whores, cured of their crabs,
miss the release their fingers brought—
a welcomed, self-granted freebie.

Whores and truckmen
live closer to their bodies than we,
but the itch is no respecter of persons:
all the hemorrhoid-afflicted, however high,
know the secret, guilty pleasure fingers provide
in some hidden room where none sees.
The burning itch attacks the ear
and instantly the pinkie probes
and prods until the sweet pain,
almost missed, subsides.
Tinea activa tickles our toesies;
plenty of time for healing powders,
meanwhile how glorious to grind the cracks,
spurring the itch to even greater intensities.

The man with an itch will learn
that however deep his grasp of the absolute,
however far he soars into the intellectual empyrean,
he is chained to a vulgar, shameless animal
seeking its innocent pleasures.
In this he is brother to the beasts.
Let him honor this slightly ridiculous kinship,
and may it keep him firmly anchored to earth,
one creature among many,
making his strange journey to the grave.

On a Comforter Stolen
From a Communal Laundry

Back to the jungle it is, then,
where each wars on all,
and where Tumac
has not yet been taught by Uwanna
that the civilized share the food,
and neither old nor young
need cower in the dark of the cave
to guard their stolen scraps.

Not for you the Hobbesian bargain;
you'll not be swallowed by a big fish,
nor sign any social contract
by which one wills the City
into existence through which
citizens wander safe along
wide esplanades and chorales
echo from churches whose
sinuous architecture curves like
the arabesques of the music.
Not for you the peaceful plains
where rich fields are ploughed
by manly men and children
sleep snug in warm beds at night.

This is a middle-income Co-Op,
for God's sake, not a refugee camp
where refuse is wealth,
cholera a grim companion,
and a warm cover all that wards off death.
Here neighbors mind others' packages
and babysit cats for vacationers.
Surely no need drove you to this?
Or is it a sign of some deeper hurt:
years without love, the loneliness

in the schoolyard, some unguessed
permutation of pain? If so, have
the comforter, a gift ungiven.

But I suspect rather an evil impulse,
the tracing of which would take us through
pear orchards and into Eden
and Eden's loss, into a cold land
of no comfort, nor even the flush
of shame to scald the ignorant heart.

THE GREAT VOID

She is gone into the great void,
a black hole whose immense grip
will not allow my heart to beat,
nor time to move in its blank denial.

I cannot look at her photos
though they are burned into my brain.
The baby in a Maine cabin's sink
which serves as a tub, her hair
aglow like a halo of gold
from the light of a kitchen window.

A little girl running on a beach,
outstretched scissoring legs
floating above the ground they will
never touch again. The young woman
casually leaning on a Roman balcony.

Each sibilant shutter's fleeting motion
freezes an instant of time flowing
endlessly into that black hole, that void,
shouting and celebrating the lie that
life moves, that the continuum of points
coalesce into a line that indexes a life.
It is a lie. It is a lie. It is a lie.

But sometimes in dreams I see her
and she talks to me and moves
in ways that are new, and I wake
in peace and sadness, released
for an instant between dream and waking
from the grip of the void, the black hole,
and time frozen forever, so cold, so bleak.

It is beyond bearing and is borne with every
breath and pulse, every joy and sorrow
that make the fleeting moments of this life,
my glorious life, that is also death.

CHIOS, 1999 / LOCKERBIE, 1988
Rachel d. Dec., 1988

In the clarity of this Greek light,
like no other on earth,
encircled by the blue Aegean,
before the green sweet figs,
the white, herb-flecked feta in its golden oil,
and the soft, caressing air that enfolds all—
that other life is like a dream.

Can we really be so weak
that our world remains whole
through that unspeakable loss?
Are we mayflies hovering our day
over the scum of some green pond
glued to the surface of things?
And then the clean grief strikes home
and the pain comes like a great relief.

LA LANTERNA, WINTER, 2007

Amid the cups and croissants,
on creaky knees, in heavy coats,
under the cold light of a March sun
we comment on the passing scene,
two old farts sure it is we, not it,
plunging below the horizon.

What do we learn? Memory fails,
bodies betray, friends die.
The silences between speech
have their own richness;
our ironic glances say,
readiness, readiness is all.

SEX AND THE CITY
(The fair one aces me out of my ride)

She should not be allowed to walk the street,
So tall and slim, her dress cut short to show
Full thighs that hold offending eyes in tow.
She'd consume me; such burning would be sweet.

Her raised hand intercepts my speeding cab.
To grant my wish ironic gods conspire
To thwart my need and cancel all desire.
She's off the street, sails swiftly by, the drab.

THE ASCETIC

Must I cease then to suck
the tit of the world,
disengage from that sweet bud
and the soft warmth
of the enveloping breast?
Now one of the heavier elements,
unstable and likely to burst,
it seems I must.

Exiled to the Siberian space
of the calorie count,
I must put away childish things
and watch all the foods of earth
rise off the table in an accelerating liftoff,
to inhabit some intergalactic void
in an expanding universe of health
and diminished girth.

Restaurants, too, must go,
that most civilized of inventions,
where an unseen kitchen god
serves his worshippers platefuls of love
aided by kindly acolytes efficiently
whisking away soiled linen and plates
replaced by gleaming goblets into which
are poured the numinous wines.
Guests, heated by the ruby fire,
contrive a ballet of words,
wit, and warmth to turn a necessity
into an act of high communion
that sacralizes the secular
and transforms a meal into a feast of love.

Now my tablemates
will be St. Simeon Stylites
who spent his life perched on a pole,
or St. Poemon who forbad his monks all wine,
or St. Dominic, a lover of the lash,
whose bloody back testified God
and contempt for the good things of earth.

These men bring in
the dry sands of the empty desert
and the hot breath of desiccation
to a bare table and hard wooden bench.
Their grim, gaunt-fleshed visages
glare as bony fingers point to the plate
of cottage cheese and greens
that passes for my lunch.

These are unlovely companions,
hard and ungiving taskmasters,
but there is no beauty either
in loose folds of flesh, sagging jowls,
rolls of bulging belly, the gross repository
of sloth, gluttony, and self-indulgence.

And as I shade my eyes from the sun
and look out across the rolling dunes,
in the far distance, like a mirage,
I see a tiny oasis beckoning,
promising cool sherbet, shady palms,
dates, figs, lamb roasted on hot coals
offered by a dusky-skinned beauty
whose smiling eyes and gestures say,
"Take, eat, you have deserved."

Who knows how long it will take
to cross those hot, empty sands,
or what perils and setbacks lie in wait?
The lives of heroes are hard
but their rewards are great.
Let the journey start.

Two Homes

A Japanese house haunts me.
All is empty space, muted earth colors.
Translucent white shoji open
onto tea hut, rock garden.
The eye is drawn to a hanging scroll
of black and gray branches
and a spot of color, the perching bird.
Beneath, two or three
bright blooms in a dish.
The room radiates tranquility
my heaving home forestalls.

The jagged outlines of stuff
create a cacophony of sight
that gives the offended eye no rest.
No wall but bears its burden
of past existence,
our insistence on connection.
No surface without mementoes,
testimony that we have been elsewhere.
Burgeoning books on every shelf.
All drawers clogged shut,
and closets like cattle cars.

The weight of all this stuff
will never anchor time.
A foolish pharaoh, I choose
to inhabit my pyramid
while still above ground.

METAMORPHOSIS (CONTINUED FROM OVID)

A rotting log leaps, great jaws agape,
and snaps the once motionless egret
honking and squawking its outrage,
beating furiously and futilely white wings
that once rowed it elegantly through the air,
as it slips slowly into that cavern
from which no Orpheus will ever emerge.
The log settles with placid grin
to await the rising sun,
and the beautiful, sleep-giving heat.

FLIES

I am no Uncle Toby
and will not share my world with flies.
Black zits mar the purity of my walls,
a hairy body floats in the milk,
a black cloud rises over a bowl.
They buzz and burn in filthy copulation.

I have come to love
the whip-like slap and splat
of the swatter.
The red smears memorialize
a job well done.

Though corpses litter the floor,
still they come. Like meanness,
like cruelty, like spite?
This is not about poetic similes
but about flies, which God created once
waking on the wrong side of the cosmos.

COUGAR AT THE WILDLIFE CONSERVANCY

It's hardly the chain-link fence
that separates him from us.
The empty blue stare
erases us and the children
noisily pressing against the pane
as he sightlessly sees
the rocky ridges and blue skies
of a land forever lost.

Recovery

The secret hidden even from you
has now been exposed;
bless the benevolent knife
that exorcised it.
The cells in their dark cave
rioting in undisciplined rout
were mad but not vicious,
and their absence now
makes you whole and hale.

Now on your couch you lie,
a deserted battlefield,
weary and scarred from struggle.

A cat crawls out of some wreckage,
licks its singed fur and stretches.
It walks off in search of food,
hungry and alive.

Baldness

It began to go
before we knew it.
A sleeping gland awoke,
secreted a corrosive substance
that flooded and bathed
the follicles in a lake of fire
that consumed them.
At the same time it lighted
other fires down below
that turned your friend's sister
into a source of shame
and your teacher's skirt
into a curtain that achingly
refused to open the show but
often seemed just about to.
And all this just when
your genetic heritage
(another of your father's failures)
was unfitting you for the struggle.
No bald Tarzan on his vine
would ever sweep Jane
off her feet and into his
hot, dark jungle nest.

PEOPLE AND PERSONALITIES

WILLEM CLAESZ. HEDA
(Seventeenth-century Dutch still-life painter)

He was in love with things
and the light that gave them life.
The glint of it on silver or glass
transformed his colored mud
to an angelic shining
that proclaimed not the Savior
but the objects of this world.
His brush wrote philosophic texts
on the convolutions of table linen,
and his reflections on pewter
mirror his mastery and our delight.
His panels, suffused in umber and gold
inhabiting a timeless space, teach us
the supernal beauty of what lies beneath our nose
but out of mind.
His works are hymns of praise.

To Lewis Dodgson

You so loved puzzles and paradoxes
that you became the best of them:
stodgy, punctilious mathematical don,
bohemian of the ateliers and theaters,
worshipper of a seven-year old girl-child
discovered on a golden afternoon that rained,
who gave late suppers alone to women
whose beautiful bodies enchanted you.
Shy and retiring stammerer whose glib tongue
made the famous your camera's subjects.
Both an innocent saint of childhood
and a pedophile on the make for prey,
the shrinks now have you on their couch,
and you are become a ravager of rabbit holes.
Lewis would have laughed; the reverend? Outraged.
You are a mystery wrapped in a grin
who sanely saw the world mad.

BERNINI'S PORTRAIT BUST OF
CARDINAL SCIPIONE BORGHESE

You view the world through dimming eyes
that have at last been filled with sight of all.
You need no Freud to know what moves man's heart,
what lusts and greed morality would gild.
You loved the pomp but felt no need to crush
the will or crucify the flesh for greater
glory of God. Not yours the dreams for which
men kill and die; you'd rather cut a deal
and end the morning's work with good red wine.

Your lovely villa was your body's body,
aglow with agate, jasper, malachite,
gold-flecked lapis, carnelian, marble.
The gods and goddesses of appetite
adorn your ceilings' blue and rosy glow,
and while you filled your house with all the wealth
and beauty of this world, your body grew
to folds of fat we see on massive chest
and neck and jowls.

You sloughed that off with each slow step
up the mountain while cheering on the rest
until you came, at last, into the Presence
Who rose, embraced you, saying, "Here's the man,
'Delight of Rome,' to help us with our task,
a banquet for the senior staff that must
go well. Beside me walk awhile and tell
your thoughts."
                And all were smiling as they passed
through waving banners into blazing light.

KATHY

So, this road ends—
photos and trinkets,
the faithful coffee cup
into the discarded cardboard box
along with the end of an age.
I remember you shy, hesitant,
the novice in a new posting,
in whose mouth butter would not melt
as you settled into the territory
of these large and possibly dangerous beasts.
In time the twinkle that flashed from your eyes
told me, this one knows,
no fool here, but too gentle
to speak what she knew.
Reticence can be a virtue
in the face of the absurd,
and kindness, always in as short supply
as copy paper in an English department,
is a gift you gave abundantly.
To this day I do not know
if you ever mastered the typing test,
the ghost that haunted you
with the persistence of damned spirits
endlessly eluding exorcism,
but I do know you breezed through
every test of the heart with flying colors.
And now you leave to bestow on other venues
that grace we thought was ours always.
No novice now but rather mother superior
whose gentle mastery we shall sorely miss.

Small Winner

I did not burn with a hard gem-like flame,
rather sputtered and funked, almost went out
but not quite.
Made no discoveries, wrote no book, made no name.
One thought I'd be a magnificent failure
but claimed I had become a mediocre success.
I nodded, dragged on the cigarette,
cocked an eye at the cards
on the green baize,
riffled the few bills in front of me
and folded the hand—
There would always be a new deal—for a while.

THE ABORTION

I am speechless.
I am closing down.
My warm dark home
is growing cold and distant.
I have no terror
but know I should.
How I know I know not,
nor how these parts
came to be nor why
the knot of me is unraveling.
The festoons of fibers
ever complicating
relax and dissolve
to the chaos I come from,
a miracle not to be.
Why this half-gift that is a curse?
I have no rage, no tears
but know I should.

SECRETARY

for M.M.C.

I have seen the troubled colleague
ensconced in the confessional of her love
receive absolution at her careful hands and
leave the quietness of her attention restored.

Or the languageless student blurt out
the agitated skein of tangled incoherence
her deft fingers weave into shining cloth
of comprehension and calm.

Each day was warmed by the shared tea
and the golden honey of her sweetness,
her lemony laughter at our follies
that pardoned as it pilloried.

In the confusion of our lives
she has shared her life with us,
a pearl of great price freely given,
a gift of grace that outlasts her absence.

DAD

You were the unpromising material
I had to shape into a father,
investing you with an authority
that would make me an obedient son.
Stubborn, unreasonable, easily hurt,
how often you tempted my cruelty,
a blank stare your only barricade
before your articulate son's onslaught.

I was not equal to the task.
I cannot count the ways I failed you.
You taught me that love was not enough,
and the ache of that lesson sears still,
though I know if I could fall weeping
into your arms, you would try to console
what you could not understand.

ASIAN INFLUENCES

FOR HAN SHAN AND THE OTHERS

Even in your day
it was a literary trope:
to resign high office
and slip away
to the high mountains,
wandering icy streams
until the very deer
would eat from your harmless hands,
the only sound
the woodcutter's invisible axe.

Mountains eternally present now
as splotches of ink on silk
where we see you, sometimes,
a tiny figure
in the immensities of mist and gorge
imperturbably lost in a waterfall's
moving stillness.

We do not aspire to it, really,
caught, as you probably were,
in the swirl of the dust of this world,
the hot dust of desire and duty,
the passions whose
weighty chains we love.

But as we read you
there grows the sad nostalgia
for the one who might have been
who walks the peaks
and drinks the clear, cold streams.

To the Tune of Falling Plum Blossoms

Late, almost too late,
I have found the life destined me.
Translating Dante and Sciascia,
teapot by my side, smoke
curling from the deadly cigarette
as the word-hoard grows
and the cello sounds Bach's
impossible profundities with ease.

On the terrace, sweeping
debris and showering thirsty plants;
the sun climbing, promising heat,
the river busy with boats,
the great gothic span strides still,
beloved panorama,
mine for the looking.

My companion of years busy
at the kitchen table
doing who knows what
with an unimaginable hoard of papers.
She will brew tea for us
and fry an egg if I ask.

Later, if luck holds, translating
from the depths of my mind
into shining phrases filling the page—
Du Fu, Li Bai, smiling at my shoulder.

If not, then to my books, so rich,
old and new, I know not where to begin,
and the chosen one then repays
with the thought that strikes to the heart,
another gift from an uncaring universe,
as prodigal as always.

Seventy years of drifting
have brought me here—how fortunate.
I have not deserved it.

TRAVEL
(after the Chinese masters)

To range the world
drinking the inexhaustible upsurgings
of the Dao;
this is good for the soul,
praiseworthy.

But to shit on one's old seat
and shower with all the familiar at hand,
this too is good,
a delight.

Summer Storm

At evening, the blossoms imbibed
an immense summer shower.
At dawn, heavy heads bend toward earth—
drunkards all.

Raga

The piercing notes of the raga
mean just what they say:

Gay runs of trilled notes course
across the scale
delivered in impossibly
rapid machine gun bursts,
staccato stops,
arabesques of mad melody,
the tabla's beat rushing behind it,
rapping and booming against
the sitar's metallic twang,
insistent, driving,
making the heart gay,
swelling the heart with joy,
bursting the heart with joy.
ineluctable, unbearable,
it cannot stop, let it never stop,
oh, wonderful sounds, never stop.

But they do—and a note,
a pure note, is born, sounds,
swells, wavers, hanging
in air and then another
that contemplates itself, glows
and fades slowly, and a third and fourth
create a wandering melody,
slow, stately, with the tabla's
soft thumps padding behind it,
searching, quivering intently,
profoundly thoughtful, sound thinking,
meditating, discovering itself—
"Sadness," it says, finally,
"I am sadness turning into a stately dance
of joy and sorrow for all that grows, blossoms,
and dies and is reborn again,

always reborn again,"
says the stately wandering dance,
the sitar's sympathetic strings
humming joyfully with the melody.
As fingers pick up the beat,
the melody finds the tonic
begins again
twanging
marching, always marching,
turning, saying:

"I am Shiva's music, and in every beat
a universe flowers and fades."
Listen as the music strolls,
casually riffs a run of notes,
handing it to the tabla,
repeats it again, strolls further,
moves ahead, moves forward,
nothing can stop its stately dance
of ecstasy through and beyond pain.

"I am Lord Shiva's music;
laugh with me, tears coursing down
your cheeks. Hear me. Dance me.
Be nothing but the dance, here, now."

SCIENCE

ENTROPY

This universe is a clock running down
no key will rewind.
Its last tick sounds eternal silence.
The stars will go out,
billions of failing torches,
fountains of light quenched
in endless cold and dark.

We and all our race
will never see the great death,
nor meet the other castaways
lost on pin-wheel galaxies,
nor learn their tongues,
nor sing the songs
they penned in praise of life.

In Praise of the Lens Grinders

How right that Spinoza,
who held nature as God,
earned his bread grinding glass.
Through his agency
and those who came after,
we see the majesty of creation:

Banded Jupiter gleams
in the eyepiece
with three shining points of light,
its moons, as a razor-sharp inky dot,
the shadow of a fourth,
crosses the giant's face.

The pale grey cloud slowly slips
into view, Orion's nebula,
a bat-like smudge of gas
in whose black heart
gleam four tiny stars
still wrapped in the swaddling dust
of the newly born.

The wind ruffles the feathers
of the Great Blue's snaky neck.
Head low, its javelin beak poised,
its reptilian eye as fixed
as the stilts it stands on
an instant before the explosion
reveals a silver shining
at the tip of its beak that tilts up,
positions its prey, and swallows it whole.

Turkey vultures soar slowly
on rising thermals,
wing tips spread like guiding fingers
as they lazily wheel and glide
on great stiff sails, searching
for the hurt, the dying, and the dead,
ready to make a clean sweep of all.

The cilia of a slipper-shaped
paramecium beat sinuously,
revolving its flanks and propelling it,
whale-like, through plankton,
its vacuoles pulsing with life.

The grinder's gift
of polished glass
corrects the mind's myopia,
obliterates size and scale.
We see our disjoint world
brought to a single focus
as if viewed by a spirit
lost in a bliss beyond time.

HOROSCOPE

It's a crock, of course,
but what a beautiful idea:
the black bowl of night
wheeling overhead,
its blazing points outline creatures
whose homes house us.
The beautiful wanderers dance
among them in a stately minuet
of conjunctions, quadratures, oppositions
caught in a natal net
whose cabalistic signs
and geometric vectors,
pregnant with meaning,
define, admonish, advise.

In this egalitarian enterprise
no untouchable outcast,
no member of a lost
Amazonian tribe, is missing
from that celestial roster.
Every house cat and pup
has a preordained fate
inscribed in the fabric
of stellar existence.
No gear turns in the vast machinery
of heaven that does not echo in us,
the darlings of creation,
the cynosure of all there is,
at the very center of everything,
giving and taking meaning
until our sun burns to a black cinder.

Deus Absconditus

In the beginning
his own hands were dirtied
making us.
Then a giver of law,
first from a mountain
and then from mathematical blueprints
hidden in a transcendent drawer
whose lock could be picked
if we were patient,
and his signature read
if not worshipped.
Now a mad woman
locked in an attic
outside time or space
or understanding,
whose antic hip
bumped our universe
into being,
where fleeing galaxies
turn red from shame or rage,
no one knows.

CONFRONTING GOD

The Abandoned Children

Our primal parents, those noble boobies,
had nothing going for them but their beauty,
no shield against the cruel and clever.
It stunned him, could not halt his endeavor
to palm off some poisoned sweets to babies.

Their sexless world taught them only ease,
tits, cunt, and prick left them in peace,
no more than the ripe peach they press
to innocent lips from boughs that never cease
to bloom nor ever feel winter's distress.

What could that futile warning signify
to them whose tongues spoke no language of loss
and never saw a shining, well-shaped lie
or smelled in it the reek of rotting corpse?
No, their world and souls were whole and one.

Their infant minds that counterfeited thought,
their cloistered virtue in an alfresco cocoon
that made them marks for what the tempter sought
estrange us from them, a breed unknown
who might as well have lived on the moon.

Of course, they would learn all too late
to see with opened eyes their fallen state,
signed by the shame their bodies wore,
bodies now objects of desire and hate,
and the seamless mind cleft forevermore.

Now they lived on common earth
and suffered the seasons of drought and dearth.
We must admit their punishment was just—
they were condemned to mirror us.
Childhood ends in Eden as all dreams must.

EVE'S SOLILOQUY

Why did I bite? That book does not tell all:
The fruit looked so luscious and smelled so sweet,
And my soft friend entwined about my waist
Had a beguiling tongue that promised much.
I was only Eden's afterthought, created
To play a servant's part and bend my will
To man's, more perfect, but this rib rebelled.
Blame me for Eden's loss and all our woe,
But all you have and are exist because
I dared to tread the path he trod, my guide,
Who spoke no lies that day nor ever since.
No Satan as say woman-hating saints,
But truth-seeker who sought to be a god.

To lord it over us, God forbade Eden
Lest we eat eternity and escape
His wrath and his great urge to deal out death.
He deemed my children's crimes as capital
And rained death on them for forty days
And nights. Burning sulphur fell on Sodom.
He hardened Pharaoh's heart to show his might
And corpses filled the land and mothers' cries.
The Chosen, at his command, labored long
To cleanse the land of Canaanites, whose sin
It was to live. When they failed, he punished.
Sorrow it is, my sons, like captives,
Came to worship their tyrant and despise
Themselves. Their mouths sing psalms to him and his
Mercy and goodness but in act they ape
His ways, and no more cruel and bloody deed
But done for him and in his name. My wise
Serpent still whispers liberty to ears
That will not hear, and I stand and weep tears
Like Rachel for her lost children, but what
Is hers compared to mine who lost all men?
He cursed my labor with a paltry pain,
As nothing to the grief that after came.

A Footnote to *Paradise Lost*

Shamed, exiled, and alone,
compassless but compelled
to divine right from wrong,
free but shackled to self-awareness,
they picked their way across
the stony desolation of their souls.

But they walked erect,
soon found a cave to hide
from cold, dark, and fear,
kindled the red flower that warmed,
shaped the stone that fed.

And he stroked her hair
as she writhed in pain
pregnant with the generations.
He looked in awe
at the red thing struggling
between her thighs, then cut it free.
Lifting it, tried to wipe away the blood
from this impossible creature,
shouted when it cried, dimly aware
that this was the first to grow tall,
to help with the hunt,
to be his heir and win this world.

THE TOWER OF BABEL

"See," he said, "what they're doing now,"
as the tower rose daily to his demesne.
"There goes the neighborhood, unless
we go down there and end it." He brooded:
It had gone wrong from the beginning—
First the woman and her doltish clod
and then her murderous son,
and my sons who could not keep their
hands off her lovely offspring,
so welcoming with thighs wide.
I should have blotted it all out
as a child clears the chalkboard
with a smear of wet rag,
the blotched mistake gone forever.

My stars blaze, the galaxies wheel
in my law. The gazelles are good,
and the lions gorging on them, obeying the law,
and all beautiful, but they are not enough;
one wearies of their placid perfection.

But was the answer a puny creature
with godlike longings? I must have thought so,
for I floated Noah on my flood
and wrote a memo in the sky lest I forget.
And here they are again with a new assault—
they are determinedly inventive, I give them that.

"Well," he said, "let's go then and do it."
And when the worker called for brick
his fellow looked at him as mad.
The foremen cursed in a thousand tongues;
the empty tower stands unfinished,
the people scattered throughout the earth.
God, in his heaven, watches for what's next.

THE GOLDEN CALF

Old habits die hard,
and comforting it is to have
one's gods continually present,
especially those celebrated
with music and feast,
drunkenness and debauch.

This new one's too forbidding,
hidden on a mountaintop in clouds
whose thunder and fire
send the youngsters
wailing to their mothers.

A lover of deserts,
and a harsh judge—
He will want too much from us,
a simple people, very like
our Egyptian neighbors,
whom we left like thieves in the night
burdened with their jewels and gold,
to enter a world girdled with
thorns and brambles
that will tear our hearts to shreds.

Now the sands cover me,
the broken shaft of my tribesman's spear
through my heart.
I am the first and show the way.

PURIFICATION

Then we burned heretics,
their ashes as clean
and pure
as their lives were not,
and their screams ascended
to heaven
as their prayers did not.

They confessed
before they died
urged on
by instruments
of persuasion,
so are their souls saved.
This is a holy work
you no longer understand.

If only the world
were a stake
and all heretics
you—
Ah, then,
what a cleansing.

The Desired

They can't get enough of us,
the old gods and goddesses.
They are besotted
by this creature made of mud,
although they are more beautiful,
more powerful, and more terrible.
They will never endure fever's drought,
the rack of the diseased organ,
the shrunken body,
the empty eye and slobber of senility,
the failure of desire, and the final
mouthful of ash called death.

What can we give them
but the smoke of burnt offerings?
What is that to nectar and ambrosia
they feast on in imagined halls
that earthly mansions palely shadow,
or to a god who exists outside dimension,
devoid of senses and passions?
Yet, if these are not forthcoming,
they grow more petulant than
a slighted teenaged girl, and their
rage knows no bound but death.

The most jealous took a whole people
for his own, and they knew no peace since.
Their slightest hesitations were blasted
with pestilence, their apostasies
raised entire nations against them;
for centuries they were outcasts
wandering the twisting lanes of dark ghettos
who could win no rest from man or god.

How empty they must seem to themselves,
facing an eternity of ennui without us.
Thus Allah ordered the angels
to bow before man, making them
the agents expressing his need.
Their lives are without significance,
for nothing they do entails consequence,
their every act but another bead
on a meandering string stretching to infinity.

Our lives give theirs a vicarious passion.
We live on the edge of a precipice always;
whether we fall commands their ceaseless gaze,
and they can no more resist usurping
our triumphs and tragedies
than iron filings the magnet's pull.
We give their lusts an edge
sharpened by the certainty of loss.
No favorite of theirs but will lose
her beauty or his strength,
giving them the gift of sorrow
and the memory of evanescent joy.

Even the justice and rectitude
they supposedly love is possible
only to frail creatures
whose acts create a finality
the gods can never know.
So Yahweh gave Job his new children,
incapable of understanding the loss
or the crime of the blind power he exulted in.

They exist outside morality as outside time,
and they create and destroy worlds
between one breath and the next.
We are merely a shadow play for them,
but our flickerings entrance them.
We are nothing but Vishnu's dream,
but we are all they've got.

Therefore, when we assemble for that final bow
and ask if they enjoyed the show
and found all to their satisfaction,
let us give them the finger that signs
our contempt for their all-powerful impotence.

THE ENLIGHTENED ONE

The sutras assure me
that I am a Buddha
drifting in darkness
blind to the truth.

Diligent seeking will free me
and restore my sight.
Loosed from attachment,
done with desire,
I will enter the light.

But this darkness is warm
so let their soft arms hold me
and firm thighs enfold me
for they are my life.

Ignorant fellow, what you call
your life is only illusion,
its pains and its joys
the source of confusion.

Of course, I reply,
any Buddha knows that.

EDEN

is the love we lose
with the first unjust blow, our first lie.
In an instant's fall into shame,
we inherit a world cleft
into us and the flaming swords.
Naked, we cover ourselves
with wealth or wisdom,
toys that will not warm.
It is a space whose contours
are defined by disappointment.
It is a hollow ache that drives the exiles
to make a home across
an unbridgeable chasm between
is and ought into which we plunge.

THE CRAFT

For Milton Gilman, Poet

Of course, I agree.
Netless poetry
full of abstractions
clogged with adjectives
will never sing.

Where is the image
that rocks language
back on its heels,
that shines
like a strand of spider web
caught in a sudden shaft of light
setting the air ablaze,
gifting weak words
with the tensile strength of steel?

Language that echoes
with the roar of a waterfall
hidden in the woods
whose sudden sight
at the turn of the trail
reveals majesty?

That, like the moon
born again from the black cloud,
spreads serenity on the face
of the dark lake?

Oh, Milton, if I only knew,
If I only knew.

POETRY

The finished poem
redeems time,
fixes the fleeting moments
in an amber jewel
whose fiery core reveals
a quintessence of meaning
preserved forever.

Mysteriously, the words pass
to the page, neither created
nor controlled by the poet.
To the Greeks
this was a beautiful woman singing
softly, her lips caressing the ear
of a rapt and joyful poet.

But the Chinese say
the Ten Thousand Things
also come from a dark mystery,
the Dao, the Way.
All nature effortlessly conforms to it.
But man,
burdened with thought,
bent by will,
must school himself to be
a desireless rock, a pliant sapling,
selfless as water
sinking below
but overcoming all.

In this state
(held but for an instant)
of no-mind divorced

from seeking or judging,
a perfect, dustless mirror,
the poet cannot put a foot wrong—
becomes a sage without wisdom,
a singing instrument
through which upwells
a song of celebration
for all that comes to be and passes,
for all the beauty and pain
of this, our perfect world.

Notes

La Selva Oscura—The dark wood in which Dante has lost his way in *Inferno*, Canto I, ll 1–3.

On a Performance of *Waiting for Godot*—Lucky is the "Knook" taken by Pozzo to beautify and enlighten his existence and who delivers such magnificent gibberish when commanded to think.

On a Comforter Stolen from a Communal Laundry—In the film *One Million BC*, Tumac, a caveman from an uncivilized hill tribe, meets, is tamed by, and falls in love with Uwanna of the sea people. Thomas Hobbes, a seventeenth-century political philosopher, wrote *Leviathan* in which he claimed "all warred on all" until man voluntarily gave up his freedom to the state in exchange for safety. The pear orchard refers to St Augustine's realization of man's unnatural state of depravity when recalling his stealing pears for the fun of it rather than to satisfy hunger.

Flies—*The Life and Opinions of Tristram Shandy* by Laurence Sterne: "Once, he [Uncle Toby] caught an overgrown fly that had tormented him cruelly all dinner-time, and he put it out the window saying, 'Go poor devil, get thee gone, why should I hurt thee?—This world surely is wide enough to hold both thee and me.'"

To Lewis Dodgson—I am indebted to Karoline Leach's *In the Shadow of the Dream Child* for this view of the writer.

Little Red Archetype—Catherine Orenstein's study of this tale, *Little Red Riding Hood Uncloaked*, illuminates the poem.

Small Winner—"To burn always with this hard, gem-like flame, to maintain this ecstasy, is success in life," Walter Pater, *Studies in the History of the Renaissance*.

For Han Shan and the Others—The last four lines of the first stanza shamelessly echo (some would say steal) lines by Du Fu and Wang Wei. Such "borrowing" is part of the Chinese poetic tradition to which I am happy to acknowledge my indebtedness.

Travel—The mystic, Lao Tzu, in the *Dao De Jing* describes "The Dao" (The Way, from which the universe springs) and man's proper relation to it.

The Abandoned Children—"I cannot praise a fugitive and cloistered virtue . . ." is from Milton's *Areopagitica*, a work advocating intellectual freedom.

Eve's Soliloquy—"Eden's loss and all our woe" is from Milton's *Paradise Lost*, of course. Who today can make assumptions about what is or is not part of the common reader's poetic experience? Obviously this great poet's epic is an important element in this poem. If you're going to steal, steal from the best.

For Milton Gilman, Poet—Robert Frost once compared writing free verse to playing tennis without a net.

Poetry—"The Ten Thousand Things" is a Chinese idiom referring to the world and all in it. The dustless mirror is from the literature of Zen.

Printed in the United States
by Baker & Taylor Publisher Services